MERIDIAN ANTHOLOGY OF CONTEMPORARY POETRY

To Anne,
Best Regards
+
Marylin Krepf

VOLUME I

MERIDIAN ANTHOLOGY
OF CONTEMPORARY POETRY

www.Meridiananthology.com

Meridian Anthology of Contemporary Poetry will appear annually in December.

It is published by NM Cyprian Publishers
904 Rose Way
Naples, FL 34104

Submission guidelines: Up to five poems. Please include: name and address on each. A stamped, self-addressed envelope should be included.

Please send submissions and subscriptions to:
MERIDIAN ANTHOLOGY OF CONTEMPORARY POETRY
P.O. BOX 970309
BOCA RATON, FL 33497

Please visit our website: www.Meridiananthology.com

Library of Congress Number: 2003102846
ISBN 0-9729014-0-X (soft cover)
ISBN 0-9729014-1-8 (hard cover)

Rachel Bentley Annual Poetry Competition

Sponsored by Meridian Anthology of Contemporary Poetry

(no rhyme please)
maximum 39 lines

FIRST PLACE
$200 featured in upcoming edition

SECOND PLACE
$50 and publication

THIRD PLACE
$25 and publication

Entry fee: $10 for three poems
Entries must be postmarked by October 1st each year.

We gratefully acknlowledge Highland Funding as a True Patron of the Arts, and we gladly welcome other benefactors.

INTRODUCTION

Welcome

This is the inaugural edition of the Meridian Anthology of Contemporary Poetry. Editors Marilyn Krepf and Phyliss L. Geller have been in the world of poetry since the 1970's.

Although our poetry is contemporary, our goal is to publish poems that reflect universal experiences and transcend the temporal and limited.

We extend our heartfelt thanks to all the excellent poets that have contributed to make this anthology a reality. We are so grateful that poets of such remarkable talent have graced our pages with their extraordinary, variegated abilities.

We wish to extend a special thank you to our production staff who helped us with all the nitty-gritty details which permitted us to focus on editing and publishing.

Patricia Foresman has worked creatively and diligently on producing a beautiful cover for our anthology. We are very appreciative of her talent and effort.

We hope you will read this anthology with the same pleasure and enthusiasm that we have had in editing and publishing it.

Phyliss L. Geller, Editor and Publisher
Marylin Krepf, Literary Editor

TABLE OF CONTENTS

The Egret Tree

A thick mist opened before our car,
a spectral river shimmering
snakeweed, bluestem, mullein,
when I saw what I thought
were white linens draped on branches
or a strange, milky fruit I'd never known.
Then the prairie sun sliced through dreaming.
We passed a man carrying a sign that read
Tulsa. You said something about egrets
hitching rides on the bony hips of cattle.

Time shimmered and spread its wings.
I imagined the yellow smudge of their beaks,
a feathery nimbus rising, air's inspiration
under outstretched wings.

In sensible light, I thought again it must have
been only white linen strewn on branches
to draw me in.

Jackie Bartley

Hermitage
(a pantoum)

I press through the foliage of a strangler fig
vines and branches form a grotto around me
a boat motors past toward the wide open bay
green water slaps against the greying dock

vines and branches form a grotto around me
the smell of smoke seeps through the leaves
green water laps against the deepening twilight
the air is sweet and dense like warm champagne

the smoke is invisible, seeping through the leaves
White Ibises step along the shore of the canal
the breeze is hot and moist with the promise of rain
a lone brown Limpkin swoops down in the middle of the flock

White Ibises strut, orange beaks flashing in unison
a boat motors past toward the wide open bay
the lone Limpkin thrusts its black beak in the ground
I press through the foliage of a strangler fig

Kathy Macdonald

The Tenth Muse

The Muse wakens, an apparition
captured on the silver surface of my mirror

I am the tenth sister, she tells me, *an outcast*
condemned by my silence and my solitude,

exiled to the edge of consciousness,
I hide from my sisters

they are frantic with the alchemy of
words and tenses, commas and metaphors,

jealous and vindictive, they have left me
blind and bereft like Thamyris,

Immortal,
they have deserted us

You are an imposter, I shout
Leave me alone

I am you, she smiles
And I have

Kathy Macdonald

Artemis Resurrected

As he starts his opening statement,
I sight him in my peripheral scope,
the smallest buck to stray so far
I unload my cache of weapons:
black cellphone, red Mont Blanc,
grey laptop, glowing certainty blue

He stumbles to the podium, trousers
stuck to the top of his socks,
in open Court without camouflage,
fumbles with his written script,
lurches back toward the cover of his table,
mesmerized by the beam of my indigo screen

I stand and sight him in my scope, dead-on
the thick sway of my shoulder length hair
falling into place, the dark rustle of silk along
my lean legs, the smart staccato of my heels

I hold him in the cross hairs, fingers clasped,
stance stalwart, never recoiling from the blast,
my hands part like two elegant butterflies
Your Honor, I begin

A contract is a sacrosanct covenant, as
ancient as man's first spoken promise
As inviolate as a man's handshake

Kathy Macdonald

After thc Fall

I'm working on what to say when the world
falls, when it slips off the edge of the half
dome like a dying wild bird. I've asked
it to trust me, to remember the quarrel
of my plagued conscience on those hunting trips
where I couldn't force myself to kill. Maybe
I'll start there, from that first shifting of leaves
after the car door was slammed, when the crisp

cool air and my father's wide smile told me
this was where we belonged, where White-tails, Pat's
and Black Bear reached back through Autumn's northern
memory, where the timber exposed the sea
of its center ring, and where our minds hiked back
through eternity's narrow trails and crosswinds.

Barry Ballard

Gravity

Here I am again sitting in the corner
of what has been a loosely defined world.
And I think, "I am still the child hurled
toward the Sun depending on a few words
that can reach and hold my gravity." I
remember the feelings of competing
with my brothers for the warmth of evenings,
for my father's words, their love, their insight.

And now my son (whose silence of the past
four years has tortured me) calls to say he
wants to get reacquainted, that somehow
in the stellar furnace his fingers have grasped
the capacity for forgiveness, a doorway eased
with grace from the mixture of light and shadow.

Barry Ballard

Elegy on a Canal Lock

"The havoc wrought in the ranks of the Irish workers by malaria and cholera almost beggars description. It has been said that one Irishman died from the disease on this project for each six feet of canal built."

– "Fort Wayne on the Old Wabash & Erie Canal"

The thick emerald clots of duckweed cling
To the cattails scratching in the thermals
Along the berm overrun with brambles,
Mica dragonflies rise on whirly wings.
The piebald bark of a sycamore rattles
While on the horizon a thunderstorm
Is blinking in heat lightning semaphores.
On the broken bank, bellowing cattle
Drinking from the canal,
Sing dirges in mournful bovine chorale.

Larvae of a thousand species wriggle
In the black smelly ooze beneath the ledge
Of crumbling towpaths, grown thick with hedges
In blossoming yellow honeysuckle.
Tadpoles break the tension of the surface
Taking their tentative metamorphic breath –
Descend into the olive-drab depths
To evolve into a croaking chorus,
And in their turn, partake
In requiems of the inarticulate.

Water no longer sluices over the weir
In the vestiges of the limestone locks.
The stagnate pool below dappled by hemlock
And cottonwoods where phantoms still appear.
Slates smoothed by a century and a half
Of heaving frost left only detritus
Of indecipherable names and dates –
Though they are known –
It's here they died with every six foot gained,
Yet, little or nothing of their feat remains here.

Barney F. McClelland

The Rooftops of Paris

"Bonjour Madame Hummingbird,"
I say, saluting with my French Roast coffee
on my third floor balcony
as the flecks of white gold
drip from the elm tree
standing between
the morning sun and me.

Her febrile darting between
The salvia and nasturtiums
now kept company
by *Monsieur* Bumblebee
pushing his pollen cart
from the back alleys,
straining the tensile pansies.

Fin-de-siècle rooftops peek
from behind the catalpa tree.
The random dormers
jutting from the black slate peaks
pose for coffee table books,
reminiscing for a city
I've never seen.

"Tigre," *mon chat, tres impatient,*
meows – his breakfast is late.
(He doesn't give a damn about the slates.)
Zut Alors! Nearly seven with much to do
My entire French vocabulary
Exhausted, I bid adieu:

"Au revoir, mes amies!"

Barney F. McClelland

In The Library Of The Mind
Pompano Beach, FL

Two palms,
like bookends,
brace the volumes before me.
There is the ocean,
bound in the black of night
and more heard than seen,
telling its tales yet below my balcony,
its white rollers but pages flipped by the tide.
The far darkness,
a further narrative,
speaks of sailors gone down to the sea,
their presence now but a green or red speck in time.
The stars above,
seen in the holes between the clouds,
are still another saga,
as is the sweep of the lighthouse beacon
and the drone of a plane unseen.
Adventure stories for all to read,
braced by the bookends of
two palms.

Brian C. Felder

Inland Waters

It still comforts me, this lake.
It will always comfort me, I think.
Its calm becomes mine when I let it in,
when I open myself to it.
This lake,
be it full of daylight or darkness
or tinges with their passage,
fills me with its serenity
and always when I need it most.
I know this lake well
but I think it knows me better.

Brian C. Felder

Final Arrangements

Your brother's death was unexpected. After all,
we understand that everybody dies
only in the way we know that people live
in Rajasthan. There — we have to make this up —

it's morning and already hot. A boy,
watched over by a silent elder brother,
adjusts, importantly, for yet another time,
the dowry in the ancient, borrowed truck:

a bolt of colored cloth, some furniture,
a spotted goat that gazes vacantly
beside the stack. The flies, unawed, tap randomly
against the rusted truck-bed, boy and goat

Yesterday: the brilliant wreaths of flowers
and dancing. Today: the cautious choreography
inside the small, dark hut, as bride and family
move awkwardly around the huge unspoken thoughts

of what will be, past Palpor and the Vindhya Range.
Who are these people and their kin? Will this small boy
*grow cruel? And what....*Outside, a thin voice
beckons, breaks, attempting husbandly authority.

Her mother presses her a cloth of honey-cakes,
gold jewelry. The younger children watch,
reverent with fear. Her father kisses her —
her caste-mark seems a solitary cloud in open sky.

This day, invisibly upon them all their lives,
is here. "Go now, child." He shifts abruptly
to the refuge of a small routine and then she turns
and steps into the terrifying light.

Richard St. John

All Souls Flight

For my Mother

Here and there, a pool of reading light
Passengers shift pillows, try to sleep.
Near eighty, you're moving toward a place
none of us has been — Iona, Ireland:
The Book of Kells. A sole page turned
each month. *If one stayed*, you say,
you'd see it all. Where saints, birds, beasts,
fish, flowers illuminate the Celtic cross.
A place of silence, stone, and waves, and stars.

Four rows ahead, a child wails —
has been howling for an hour.
Nothing can comfort it. Its pure cry of want
makes the whole plane uneasy in its wish,
its inability to quite forgive
that raveled howl. But you think only
of the child. You go to help. You touch
the mother's shoulder with a quiet palm.
No, there's nothing you can do. You sit again.
A stewardess steps past you in the dark.

Now I imagine you think of us, the souls
you helped bring up. Babies. Beasts.
Those years. The Book of Kells, and where
the manuscript breaks off. The waves
invisibly beneath you, rushing past.
You drift. You almost sleep. Headed toward morning
with that earthly keening in your ears.

Richard St. John

For a Friend Turning Thirty

I

We can learn from these Dutch still lifes
in Toledo, Ohio. In the handle of that knife
resides the weight of hundreds of others
held and set aside, seen and remembered,
rendered and rerendered, seen. It takes an eye
you don't have at eighteen to paint like this.

II

The essential thing is not that these pieces
found their way to a museum, grabbed a spot
in art history, but rather the rightness
of this light, spilling through a goblet
and onto a linen cloth; one's sense
that the curve of this pewter platter had to be.

What counted most for these Calvanists
was faithfulness — in the even grinding
of pigment on stone, in the welcome of houseguests
with cordials in the afternoon, in thanks
for the breadth of sky above a harbor —
the faithfulness of hand and heart and eye.

III

And see, the achievement here embraces
domesticity. The brushes in that greystone jar
are no more prominent than this wooden bowl
or dented kitchen spoon. This unplatonic
vision seems equally at home with fresh cut
flowers or page-ends, or with half-carved meat.

IV

Then there's Toledo, the kind of town
we all grow up in. Famous, in a smallway,
for fiberglass. Its sights familiar
as our signatures — the plastic wading pools
in our backyards, our powermowers, the glare
from off our cars on these midwestern streets.

Just blocks from the Owens-Corning Tower
in a building cleaner than it ought to look,
with Bunny Bread transit benches out front
and sporting an overly-manicured lawn,
we find these works of grace — incongruous
and unexpected. And yet, undeniably, here.

Richard St. John

In the Middle of the Lake

The canoe bobs on the lake.
A few light waves lap against
the sides trying to turn it,
sink it, but the water's own depth
slaps down such freshness,
holds it aloft.

My thoughts drop anchor.
I leave the voyage to the
rough-hewn paddles, to a
callus or two that scale
my palms, an ache in some
distant leg bone.

For here, my head doesn't know my body.
My face feeds off
the gentle briskness of the wind.
My blood is like tides rolling
back and forth to
the steady moon of my heart.

John Grey

First Child

It is while observing
the sudden landing
the ratchet-like connection
of bird to branch.

There is no point in watching the swell of your belly
or listening to the echo
crying deep inside you.

Birds cling to the
thin, swaying limb,
the farthest outpost of all being.
Birds covet clouds,
defy rain.
Birds soar out of
the forest's thick green uterus.
Birds fly and fly
to bless the moment
they get airborne.

John Grey

What Was

Not done
Remains
After
What is
Or was
Is gone.

Edward Michael O'Durr Supranowicz

The Marble Tomb to Crown Life

It was caused by nothing,
aimed at nothing but popular outrage.
Frustration, discontent, unrest...
all these offsprings
of the disabled single party rule
are now issuing their pervasive yells
all around the new and the same old country
caught up in complex implications
of its discarded but
thoroughly tenacious past.

The unknown present day
breaks in upon the petrifications
of what has been sanctified
by the multitudes of the ever-marching
purple, red, bloodstained, bleeding
banners now carried high
by the staunch advocates
of the good old totalitarian days.

Their lofty calls
seem to fail to chime
with the somewhat less lofty
cries of those butchered
in Stalin's prison cells,
now wafted to the marcher's ears
from the cells of their own lingering memories...
The marching former convicts
crave for Stalin whose much lamented death

let them out of the prison cells
but buried them
in those of their wounded souls...
Are these parading relics just the guns
Stalin triggers off
from under his marble tomb?
The marchers never question.
They are called up from the past
and are here to obey.

Vladimir Orlov

Caged Garden of Life

In a gloomy garden of the golden cages
suspended on the golden chains
at the whim of a wistful gardener,
trees of a quashed joy rustle alive,
alive to the roaring wind rudely stripping them
of their yellow apparel of an anticipated slumber.
Lawns of gilt offer their own
rampaging yellow, lawns of a decaying life
stifled to death by the marauding weeds.
The whole garden is an ungainly cage
of rust which is the gold's aftermath.

Vladimir Orlov

I Will Send My Message Collect

I will send them all the torn-out copies
of my last message collect,
as I stand breathing in the sight
of the frozen silver, its faulty light
fettering the river's glassy ice.
My memory, in its inveterate longing
to plunge into the sweet water of hope,
is being thrown to the gusty summit
where regiments of ghastly ghosts gather
to perpetrate their ghoulish parade.
Time rumbles down the bumpy street
of my crumbling consciousness, as
I am being effectively run down by its heavy cart
which used to stop at my beck and call before,
but which now will positively not,
even if I vociferously plead with it.
Days are being sipped out of me,
with relish, by the subtle connoisseurs
of the delicious wine of time and age.
I will send them all the torn-out copies
of my last message collect.

Vladimir Orlov

In Limbo

Pearl hat pins mark my husband's trail on a map I finger,
like tracing his square jaw. I stab Soon-Tek, six thousand miles
away where he last camped and mailed a cassette.
I drink green tea, listen to his voice.

Death every day. This morning the sergeant held up his trophy
strung on a wire, two bloody human ears...

My corgi whimpers for a run in the woods. Go on, I open the door.
Snow is falling. Pop screamed at breakfast, *damn mutt! I'll kill it!*
Fur sheds on his Barcolounger. He's angry because a rice paddy mine
blew off my brother's right arm and ear.

By afternoon the snow buries rust mums like wounds in the garden.
I miss the dog, walk past the pottery shop, its graveyard of lawn statues
in limbo till summer. There she is, crouched behind a boy on a dolphin,
snow sticking to their faces.

Pop drives the *damn bitch* to the pound after the evening news
and coffee with floating dog hairs. I live in this house until 'Nam
is over, have strength enough these days only to imagine clawing
out his eyes. I turn on the tape.

When I'm trying to fall asleep at night with the crack-crack of
snipers' fire,
I think of you, sketching Hetty in Pop's chair...The monsoon is coming,
a hot wind
from the mountains lifting white dust that clings to trees, rifles, flesh.

Zan Gay

The Larch Tree Swastika

Fall needles brown the swastika
mountain villagers see below each year
in the green conifer forest, wounding

a landscape trying to forget.
An eyesore among lakes and heaths,
despite summer attempts

to slash the pattern, dispelling
the Fuehrer's ghost. The trees grow back
keeping the mystery why a forester

sixty-odd years ago planted the trees:
compliance to higher orders?
a patriotic lark?

It is time, the villagers cry.
Now chain saws break the morning
silence, felling all larch trees that bloody

blue skies, spilling sunlight at last
into places where children
might have played, had they not

been shoved into trains,
the forester never hearing their songs
while they picnicked on ripe yellow plums.

The fallen trees pile up, stripped logs,
stacked cords of wood thrown
into kitchen ovens for baking honey bread.

Zan Gay

Slow Take

Hidden hunger
hangs about my being
like a craving for citrus
or some greens,
forcing me to notice
it's been a while
since I heard from you.

I hear the even beat
of your continuo
on Blondie — your bass viol
smell the peanut butter
spread across the mornings
of your childhood
see your lovely wife
reach toward you with a kiss
and feel a missing link.

You're busy
tired, overworked
need some time to rest.
Excuses flow like mother's milk.
Sucked dry
sore spots grow —
hurt feelings, anger, pouts
threats of getting even
till the ulcer bursts in recognition
it's not grapes or South Africa
being boycotted it's me
and I am left to feel my hunger
turn to pain.

Cherise Wyneken

Eruptions

Buried anger seethes
beneath tectonic plates
of mind.
Bank and cover.
Bank and cover coals —
feelings that inflame.
How long must I abide
this walking rule book man?

Hot fumaroles
heave up humid steam.
In a burst of lava
blistered words erupt —
"I hate you!"
Shocked into stillness
like cindered after flow,
my fired feelings
melt his rigid core.
He has no rule for this.
Only, *"Why?"*

St. Helens' wooded slopes
laid bare
we dare to talk.
Tiny tufts of grass
begin to sprout —
baby's hair
on balded land.
A kiss — bedded lava flow,
banks and covers.
banks and covers coals.

Cherise Wyneken

Tell Me Your Life

Like a poem seeded in giant flowers facing
sunlight, long-blossomed shoots come
to the end of their branches, fly through
solar roofs, into ether.

Dreams propel sisters. Seeds cocooned in silken
sheathes, bud, flower, spin and tumble in the fog.
Dying petals fall to dried earth in shock wave drag.

Do epiphanies arrive full-blown
from sleep states, hear the heart beat
under an avalanche of doubt, or do they
inch-dance, then mile-leap into space?

Spurred by desire, the seed of flight,
poets drift toward wind tunnels, while sisters
who first dream, flower in the open sky.

Lucille Gang Shulklapper

Freshly Pained Walls of Lemon-Yellow

Limping along the hospital corridor
glossy as sunshine through rain
the Cuban woman's red lips

curve sunshine to
the nurses   the doctors
the faces   she passes

almost out the revolving
door   into the Miami
heat   her mouth yellows

I think she says
I am rain.

Lucille Gang Shulklapper

Room 27: Alzheimer Unit

My mother-in-law mother,
the blackest figure in the waiting

room window, looks out into
the corpse of a beached

storm; its body parts of memory
strewn...a legless sandpiper,

a dying shark with eyes
like specks of sea glass

washed ashore. Helen, you
stand legless, your sea glass

eyes stare into the burning sun,
obscured by thunderstorms,

matted and framed; do you
know that you are backlit

by the parched light of love?

Lucille Gang Shulklapper

When I Was Alive

Those were the days
the sun shone hot on my neck and shoulders
I walked down the dirt road
branches overhead waving away the layers of languid heat
water cool and bracing as I swam in the snapping river
it was wonderful when I was alive
my super-heated body probing supple flesh
explosions coursing through my fevered brain
those were the incredible days
children with their eyes wide and glistening
ecstatic as they jumped into the joyous water
rushing along the deck to throw their wet arms around me
revealing the glories of unqualified love
I glimpsed the future with its rainbow halo
marvelous when I was alive
the lattice-work memories piling one on top of another
we placed the rocks and made a campfire grilling hamburgers
sizzling juicy hot dogs cooking sweet corn in great pots
roasted potatoes drank cold beer and swigged tart wine
it was perfect to be alive
the way I recall it
nothing to compare
I would tell blatant tales to enthused audiences
reveling in the puffs of excitement
thrilled to the glowing strains of grand opera
enthralled by the spun gold of scribes and poets
tingled before the canvasses of the impassioned painters
rejoiced in the great pleasure of being alive
that was the way it seemed
but not here
where it is strangely silent and passionless
but perhaps this too is a story to tell.

Gerald Zipper

227 Santa Margarita Street, Lima, Perú

Across the street a gardener works
bent double to his task pulling
clumps of weeds from the earth.
Two kitchen maids in blue uniform
stop to chat, then pass. Late day,
Santa Margarita's backstreet
well-tended, stately, deserted until

the bread-man pedals through startling
solitude with the discordant shriek
of his whistle. A foreigner's Sunday,
gray as a New York November.
Time now to go unpack
the heavy suitcase filled
with my own fled secrets.

From a Balcony, Overlooking a Lush Garden

Plants, trees, wildflowers,
Once disregarded now seem vital.
Dappled greens and purples
Everywhere...Bougainvilla?
Wisteria? Jessamine?

Once, some cone-shaped lilacs
Hung from an unnamed tree
Outside a hospital window
Wishing good health to me
When breezes bent them.
The naming
Of the floral world
Leafage, brush, or blossoms
Seems proper. If only just
To thank them

Brenda Serotte

Home Depot

Do we ever really know as kids
What work our fathers do?
Now I understand at last
walking through Home Depot.

Row after row of brassed, tall lamps
with conical shades we called "Chinese hats"
polished and burnished until enhanced
from dull to a lustrous bronze...

so *that's* what he did, he polished metal!
A job I couldn't articulate
I knew he worked in a factory
he left at six, we were all asleep

I just couldn't explain what it was he *did*:
He brings home big, bulky packages...
gleaming-gold filagree ash trays, round,
and also in autumn's shape

shined to the fine tips of every stem
placed here and there for cigarettes.
Who could have known their worth
or the work that went into finishing them?

Who had time to admire the useful things
forged from distant, ferocious machines,
we thought they were born that way.
Desk lamps, pole lamps, banker's lamps, trays

offered to dentists in lieu of payment,
gift-wrapped for relatives' important functions:
confirmations, graduations, a friend's
anniversary, a doctor's visit.

His ceaseless lathe lit the whole neighborhood
but neither my brother nor I understood
what it was he did for a living
and the way he dressed gave nothing away

always a suit, a white shirt, a fedora.
Decades later the words "Labor Day"
made sense. Likewise, the value
of things hand-crafted, and

the true definition of light. Tonight
when I throw the halogen switch
on the torch-lamp I bought at Home Depot
my surroundings will brighten, familiar and real

I'll feel once again that rough brush of a
beard on my cheek as I lay half asleep
in the orangey glow
of a tenement bedroom
just before lights go out.

Brenda Serotte

Sour

I eat the canning plums that
Only the birds will eat.
The soft flesh, the deep purple
Skin hiding a yellow interior.
It's like a house that
Doesn't match, like a person
With an ugly personality and a
Beautiful face. I eat plums and
Spit out the pits, projectile
Motion in action —

I've taken too much physics in school.

Pier Hart

Night Train

Far off and secret, sepulchered,
But sounding in our blood, vibrating
In our shinbones, the frightening,
Mesmerizing song of the express
Still coming fast and urgent, full speed,
Hell bent, hissing and clattering.
We wait in the dark for
The cyclops light to round
The bend, dazzle us with fear
And elation, and wanderlust
As it parts the darkness,
Rushes past our house, then,
In a minute, past the town's
Darkened, unpeopled depot.
Beneath the arches of our feet
Comes the wild, bewitching tempo
As sharp as sleet, and
The wheedling seduction:
Come...let us dream...and disappear.

The train comes snorting, swerving,
Breathing like a bull, lurching
Through the glamorous, thundering night.
We glimpse the red bandanna.
We wave as it passes in a crimson
Smudge, and the wave comes back
Big-voiced and generous:
Now it is only the dark
That lurches and swerves.
The empty tracks lie a-glimmer,
Too much awake to think of sleep,
We wait for the next faint click
In the night, the song
That only we who love a train
Can hear or understand,
Far off and secret, sepulchered.

June Owens

Rubics

Piano-fingered rain plays
in the puddles of the road,
ad libs arpeggios
on this windowpane
where I stare and wait.

Harp-voiced sprinkles pluck
at petioles of poplar leaves,
plink from the eaves
of this porch where
I rock and wait.

Close to the locking
of the day when I, in my
bewilderment, turn away toward
night, the sun flows forth,
the road goes gold,
there are rubies
in the trees;
but you are
the only jewel
my glad heart sees.

June Owens

Watching Homicide On TV Before It Got Itself Murdered

ply
wood
windows
eye stoned
brown buildings
dreams erect
churches under
peens of
music hammers

noise makes
gargoyles in
our cathedral brains
like a rude
finger a
steeple punctures
thick day's
tough membrane

echo-siren-
slick-wet zone
6 baltimore
nails crimes
to pavement
crosses as
though they
were thieves
either side
of Christ
while I
build houses
of cards

June Owens

neck trouble

a light stilled in headphone silence
decreed the trouble well worth it
from a certain angle

granted your head was turned
which would be almost enough
to justify an extra pillow

in different circumstances
the way the light struck your face
through a broken windowpane

might have spun the distance on its heel
in a nuclear family winter
then would it have doubled or doubled back

as elusive as that blind spot that appears
when you close your eyes and look slightly away

Pete Lee

An Ideal World

I wake up each morning in love with the world.
Maybe it's because my dreams teem with images

rather than ideals. Or maybe it's because dream-
images *represent* ideals (though one would hardly

consider this in the middle of a dream), something
this world – outside of a poem – just can't offer.

Last night it was a shape moving underwater,
seen from above as I lay on a narrow plank

stretched across two sections of a decrepit pier.
This isn't something one would normally fall in

love with, granted, unless one were a marine
biologist or a harbor seal: it's simply the image

I last awoke from. Then I turned on the coffee,
headed for my desk, sat down..and am now

touching up this love poem to a world I want
to last forever: an ideal world, one with me in it.

Pete Lee

Black, White and Blue

Ray Charles plays piano,
Georgia, Georgia, on my mind,
black and white ivories sing the blues,
the blues, birth of the blues.

Red blood flows,
baby cries
in black, starless night;
wiggly, squiggly crack baby,

name her Georgia,
born to be blue.

Oh Ray, pound your fingers
on that piano;
when you hear Georgia's wail
your sun-glassed eyes

see pigtails,
pinafores,
patent leather shoes;

this Georgia is
gaunt, grey,
guiltless.

Yeah, Ray,
play that eighty-eight,

sing,
pray for Georgia.

Gilda Kreuter

Flowers

Water the soil for a seed
that with a little sunlight
turns into a rose or lilac;
miraculously it knows
what to become.

And the people are here;
souls like the stems of flowers
searching and seeking in roots too.

Flowers, flowers, everywhere,
hopefully, thoughtfully, please;
like the wise little seed.

Craig Arnel

Meditation

one cloud
                    is the sky
one raindrop
                    is the storm
one slick stone
                    the slippery slope
one trunk
                    the matchstick forest
one wildflower
                    the meadow's pleated skirt
one pair of wings
                    the rising of birds
one snout, sniffing
                    the menagerie of mammals
one child, hungry
                    the fat belly of man
one prayer, uttered
                    the universe, listening

Stephen Kopel

Oncoming Night

I gaze at the horizon at sunset,
huge billowing clouds brilliant and tinged with red,
the sea churning — rosy tints capturing its crests.

Gently the sun lowers itself below the
barely discernible line between sea and sky.

My eyes roam across this great expanse
and in my heart I cry.

The beauty of this scene overwhelms me.

Hypnotically, through misty eyes, I'm held by its majesty
now in deep crimson and velvet-purple hues.

In a dreamlike reverie, I watch and wait.

Time seems endless — the sky seems darker.
The clouds glow deeper purple,
breathless, windless — awaiting the
oncoming night.

Lee Chanin

Wind and Waves

Roaring and tumbling, the ocean races toward the shore
while the storm rages.

I watch from the comfort of my room high above the sea,
intrigued by the power and surge,
swept up in its immensity.

I am safe, yet sensing danger.
The sea is hypnotic and frightening,
as its swells rumble over the beach,
foaming, spreading, then dying.

The wind's intensity hastens the billowing surf to its end,
stirring up needles of sand,
sending them whipping about.

I stand mesmerized as the fierce wind and waves slowing
erode the helpless beach.

Lee Chanin

In thc Woods...Early Spring

Sounds, they're all connected
to some memory. We're drugged with
familiarity.
A bird flies in closer. The wind

blows. Dried grasses sway. Frogs
peep. Silence. A fly speaks in the
passing. Dead leaves rattle
their carcasses amongst the blossoms.

He now sings for her. Hush.
She makes love to him. It is
inevitable, in
the beginning, all lives renewed.

Here Comes the Rain

and the winds, faster and faster,
beyond the sun's comprehension,
he peeks from behind a cloud and
the wind charges in anger and
the rains descend and the leaves clap
and the redbird clutches onto
one, tiny, braided finger, see-
sawing, syncronicity, all.

A Crow's Lament

It affects me so, to hear them.
It all begins with one, he cries
like no other creature. It is
he who can open that door, walk
into my soul, mourn with me,
console me, he, conjures up the
truth. We do not cry alone.

Therese Bearse

Shadeflowers

The window overlooks
a yard that blooms with

empty mason jars and
rusty bedsprings curled

in downward spirals. Clumps
of earth grow brittle shards

dull with city soot and gray
shadows of surrounding

brownstones. Here
Lashanda pokes holes

with a broken pencil,
filling each with black

striped seeds. She pats
the dry soil, spits

on every mound and
plants the pencil too,

a yellow signpost
to the harvest,
to hope.

Riva Dunaief

The Radio

After the War, the Allies
left their jeeps in France.
They became objects
of veneration, the carriages
of saints and saviors, kept in perfect condition,
polished like relics,
and driven out for parades
to celebrate the Liberation.

This year, young men
from my in-laws' village
dressed as American soldiers
drove them in stately procession.

In one village,
an old woman rushed
from her house,
and caressing the hand
of one startled driver,
thanked him for saving
her village, her country,
tears falling from her cheeks
as she kissed his hands.

He sat frozen, red-faced,
the other young men
smirking, stifling laughter,
the confused old dear
pouring tears of gratitude,
kneeling as if before a saint.

Finally, a niece held her back,
cooed as if to a child
awakened in a strange room;
a radio, blaring in one jeep,
was switched off.

Robert Cooperman

Clock

Though never wanting
to expose them, a truth
ferret inside me thinks
older people are trying
to fool me, have given
up, or swallowed a bill
of goods when saying
they're more relaxed
and take things easier
as they age because my
experience has been
the opposite, relaxed
as a child—summers
of long days, stomach
and elbows on vacant-
lot wild oats watching
ant-crawl, starling-flit,
and sun-mote drift
or playing Monopoly
on redwood imitation
Green-and-Green swing
porches for five hours
easy, so accepting
of friends—whereas
now, time rushes me
and I can't bear talking
with one person
for more than ten
minutes at a cocktail
party before nervously
moving on to others—
partly because of knowing
infinitely so much more
about myself, them,
history, the future,
and how fast my clock
runs.

Anselm Brocki

Camping by the Lake

On the little lake buried beneath
cottonwoods, the boats throw
waves in circles until our eyes
spin out of focus, and the sun sets.
No one notices the cause and effect
between the whirlpool,
the disappearance of the sun
and boats, and the sudden calm.
The spray of stars exists
in two places at once.
In the dark, we drink beer
and stare into the fire,
wait for the shadows to creep
behind our eyes so we can crawl
into sleeping bags. Steady breath
adds to night sighs through leaves,
and the lap of waves against shore.
Somewhere among the trees
lurks the memory of when
this sound came every night.
Light followed flames
and we could not escape
the wind over the fire
just barely controlled
that now rage only beyond
the red horizon of our dreams.

Richard Dinges, Jr.

Guardian of our Garden

The yard lies quiet under a clouded sky,
a gray hood over a still green patch.
She wanders along the edge from bush
to bush to potted plant, follows
the path of bees and a humming bird,
to gather nectar through her eyes.
I wait for a smile,
that does not come,
to open the sky to another sun.
Even the glint of her gaze
saves something of beauty
and not the craggy lines of my face.
I can only sit and wait
for my bloom long since hidden
to reappear in the memory
only she has saved.

Morning Music

Mystic static
clings to the radio speaker
between stations before
the alarm erupts
into morning dark fog
and sweaty sheets,
that moist sponge between
the gums.

A sonic boom
rattles shingles and plays
xylophone on cupboard
dishes, until the dog chain
sings at the backdoor
when the dog yaps and screen
door slaps shut.

Always muted
chatter below floorboards
of those others in this house,
while I listen to their rhythm
and tap my feet until I get
the beat and keep time
with my own pulse.

Richard Dinges, Jr.

In the Cypress Gardens

The dust is heavy. There is a ghost in the landscape.
All of life moves toward orange. The sky so
heavy it might fall. A yellow dog walks away
from the setting sun. Crows edge the sky.
Buzzards roost and fall asleep.

In Oxford Cemetary

You thought because
the trees moved
and the stones didn't
you understood
the meaning of the wind.

Louis Bourgeois

Rude Awakening

"Slam!"
Intrudes the rainy afternoon, as the
Bent black-suited renter
Retrieves his

Groceries from the
Yellow
Taxi

Kent Clair Chamberlain

Portrait of a Woman

On a mahogany table,
on a scarf embroidered with flowers,
by her mother, Leah, now gone,
rests a semi-circle of three small portraits, oval shaped,
three generations of women.
Leah, Marsha her daughter, now a grandmother,
standing in this room,
and Karen, Marsha's daughter.
Each face captures the high expectations
of a sixteen year old, of peach blossom complexion,
eyes dreamy, starry....
Leah, married at eighteen,
earth mother, baker of breads, gardener, comforter,
Marsha buried her love of theatre for teaching,
Karen, passionate for sculpture and painting.
In Leah's pink-fluted bowl nearby, full of pears,
grapes, oranges, plums, some fruit is tumbling over.

Life and stories.... Marsha marvels at it all
as she bends over the table....
cameos and flowers, fruits and dreams.
My dream was theatre, she thinks,
and so it was and is;
my students, myself, my daughter, my mother.
Pastels and eyes and brightness and sighs,
moving and waiting in this wonder.

Betty Fleischman

New Hampshire, You Knew Me

In search for a thin root from my rural past,
my map of this city has narrowed —
to thrift shops, second hand shops.
Wasn't it yesterday that I heard
a farm hand urge his team to the hay field?
Bluebirds, roosters, cowbells,
Boston and Maine's night train
whistling along our ox-bow river valley.
That is how our day was
and when seasons changed, as they must,
we searched for violets
in March's last snows.

New Hampshire, you knew me.
Your wooded trails, granite quarries,
lakes, streams, corn fields
elated my consciousness;
the Old Man of the Mountains,
the Mother of Rivers...

My hands are now wrinkled and weary,
entangled in shopping bags
in search of New hampshire trinkets, collectibles.
In my apartment my dim eyes turn
to a horse-shaped clock, my father's wind-up clock,
near the kitchen sink,
towels with cows munching hay,
a sculpture of a rooster,
as my eyes awake in the morning.

New Hampshire, you knew me.
Why did I leave you?
I never really left you, completely.

Betty Fleischman

American Outback

After all the deadlines, f/stops, bangkok
to Belem, film saturated with foreign colors,
he craves blue in his lungs,
his old migratory route
where Gaia's great bellows blow. Where he
is the only lens, and light readings fly up
like cactus wrens.

Tollways vanish in a chuckwalla's crevice.
A spring coyote flings itself leanly
into the chase of shadows, silent as a star shooting.
Custom-made cacophony is lost under the humps
of hogans listening to Venus rising.

The ripe moon mounts an agate steeple,
hailing the appointed time for celebrants
of some ancient rite his cells seem to remember.

He inhales morning's turquoise horizons
unscaled by tall containers stacked
by corporate cliff dwellers. He moves through
granite halls posing for the centuries,
staging endless similes, enclosing nothing
but samples of light
and a lone hawk's two-note keening.
Old angers slough off like snakeskin.
He looks for the shine and sharp of obsidian,
touches pinyon and a sweating pinto.

Leaving, he turns to stare at pronghorns
as they wheel back to stare at him,
freezing in last year's pose on the same rise.

Undiluted azure anoints him now,
his mouth tastes of last night's royal.
The crimped mass of wires within him
loosens like the brittle clench

of a resurrection plant greening open in rain.

Glenna Holloway

— The Sow's Ear Poetry Review, March, 1998

Night at War

Life is now a fine line.

The Baton waves
in the dark.
Death awaits
As a dog waits for a dog

Right Freedom
Left Death
TOO old
TOO young

WRONG MOVE
BAM
YOU'R DEAD
Or are you?

We are now
Walking
In
Hell

Shots in the distance
Gates open
Free
We listen
Free at last
We learn?

John Michael Buscemi

Colorado Springs, 1967
for my father

Thrown from a car window
into enormous sky
you thought you could fly
like this forever —
but forever takes decades to resolve.

You were dying
and everyone went to see you
except me

not knowing how to turn
the record over on the player
you bought me

or where Colorado Springs
even was.

Wrapped in a white blanket
lowered out the back of an airplane,
your shaved head explained
a vice-president
learning to tie his shoes,
crawling up steps
in the house on Elmwood Avenue —
your silence was rage.

Deep sea fishing off Cape Ann
we ran into a school of mackeral;
iridescent lures calling rainbowed fish —
prisms under water.

Living with less and less
I kept adding more string;
believing if my kite could touch the clouds
you would not unspool.

In a world made of yellow and blue
around which our lives spin

how small but great things are.

Stacie M. Kiner

For the Dead Come Back

I want to live with a Union Dead.
Love a man buried
one hundred and thirty years,
rising out of Richmond's ashes.

When the phone rings it's never for me.
People forget I'm living on some corner,
quietly dreaming corn.
Ripe, yellow, taller than my head
singing in the dry breeze;
a thousand miles away.

After we're dead
do people forget we've lived —
forget about men
whose uniforms hang in airless cases,
their love letters exposed,
pocket watches, train schedules —
one running hell and back
every four hours?

But these men couldn't have lived.
Hearts heavy with buckshot.
Women still waiting
on their love letters.
Mothers cursing Virginia, Tennessee, America.

Mothers calling to God
from their front porches:
mercy and corn dancing in the wind.

Stacie M. Kiner
©Apalachee Quarterly

September Eleventh

I saw the airplanes on the T.V,
my eyes indifferent as the towers fell.
After all, King Kong will
scratch his way into the frame,
a gasping Hollywood bombshell
tucked under his hairy limb, I thought.

Just about to change the channel – a panic seized me
as my eyes moved from light to dark.
Seven Jihad virgins fell crying from the sky
and the damned devil of a dragon
smoked the living breath
out of all of them.

No commercials about the one- man- band gym
or investing in futures.
Dying in the coffee break,
gasping, confessing,
closing not sweetly those petals.

I ran outside hoping to catch some one,
even though I'm in Florida,
to say "let's have some toast and tea now
and sit under a palm to relax".
But each one slipped through my fingers
as I wept and wept, arms extended to the sky.

Marylin Krepf

I Believe in Blood in a Rain that Melts the Dead

I dreamed of love
in a foolish way,
the essence of cold purpose,
what one thinks of as happy
and nothing kisses the night.

Watch my fingers.
Here is the black
geometric of time.
We are in a small room,
the wind and the rain
have just begun.
In this hour is a miracle.
The lunatics of greed,
the absurd last desire
that reappears every minute,
ceases. It is quiet.

The only real magician
is at the door. You open it.
Out of his hat comes
a flower.
He pours some water in a vase
and it turns red.
Two white gloves in the air.
You expect him to bow and leave
but he doesn't.
His shirt and his hands
turn red too.
He seems to be in great pain.

Something stirs.
You begin to consider
that you are not God.
He smiles and vanishes.

Later you listen to a minstrel.
He has wandered
his way
to your soul.

Marylin Krepf

Soul's Resilience

How sweet the rarefied air
of mountain beginnings.
How a few words of light
birthed a condensation,
eased into a stream,
surefootedly followed
the pebbled pitch of gravity,
danced around obstinate boulders
with but small ripples.

How stream has turned to river
with shifting bed too deep, too broad.
How the lies
lying fully clothed
in each the other's stranger mind
have made a muddy eddy
between two slippery banks.

How light may not be known
but for the shadows come.
How autumn bleeds into winter.
How the willingness to carry on
feeds the soul's slow struggle.
What a rose of light returns.
Oh how the spring leaps again
from shadow winter snows.

Jamie Cavanagh

Love Alone Succeeds

Flowers in the graveyard thrive.
Blood from bone to dust become
speaks memories in fragrance.
No applause attends the fight
behind unblinking rigid eyes
to speak encrypted messages.

Fathers' sons
stand or fall on their own:
not deep enough the root in tap,
not deep enough
to feed upon a father's strength,
to ease into the weakness bound
behind unblinking rigid eyes.
Love alone succeeds the night.

And the flowers look quite lovely,
tremble slightly in the breeze,
a breeze with the hint of melody —
vague tune, muffled licks.
Or is it a tremor of dust?
One postulate stands the test —
this love succeeds the night.

I knew you before the fear.
I knew you before
the old Irish songs
turned to a belly of screams —
hushed echoes of Galway Bay
faded as the wasting dance began.

Love is an easy word to inscribe,
easy to erode;
but your wordless love, my friend, is kept,
kept within this singing vault,
outlasts all the writing on stone.
Your love succeeds the night.

Jamie Cavanagh

Premonition in the Mental Hospital

The pain is so deep.
You can't even touch it.
"The numbness, the numbness, Rochelle."
She used to call out to me
From her tomb of a bed.

I could not see it.
Her outstretched leg
Looked unremarkable.
"The numbness, the numbness," she said.
"Look—"

I saw nothing of the rigor mortis.
I couldn't imagine feeling nothing.
It made no sense.
If her leg were truly numb
Why did it trouble her so?

Why did she tremble
With the trepidation
Of a lost lamb
Glimpsing the shadow of the wolf
Up ahead?

Rochelle Hope Mehr

The News

The tears came,
Blurring the words
On the paper before me.

But the tears are inside now
Where they are felt but not seen.

I know they are there
Because my thoughts are distorted
Like images seen through
A rain-drenched pane.

Shock

People are talking to me,
But I cannot answer.

I am back in a small room,
Standing by a desk,
With my glasses off.

Virginia Artrip Snyder

Flight

The moon cleave's the passage,
allowing darkness to greet light,
carrying a positive cosmic energy.

The sun rapidly filters through
an appealing aperture with a
bouncing ball ferocity.

My feet dangle from the battered
beach chair, digging deep into the
soundless sand.

I consume nature as she dances across
white capped waves, softly, swiftly.
My melancholy mood, mocking seagulls.

Their flight respected as I gaze toward
white wings flying into cotton ball clouds.
Silver gray feathers gracefully moving forward.

Spring is the proper time for healing old
sorrows. I allow this time to shed layers
of gloom as the salty air restores my peace.

Colleen Ann Traphagen

My Friend John

his hands and eyes are artists
he sees in people's heads
yesterday he moved his finger
his brain may be functioning
it's difficult to tell

he is widely acquainted
and recognizes no one

when his eyes are open
he sees the invisible
he can open them a bit
and he sees nothing

he looked forward to his Spain trip
he'll remember nothing of it
he can't move air in or out

not sure that he could hear me
I touched his arm with powdered gloves
he displays bright quilts for many friends

that car must have been doing sixty
the Chaplain was there too
yesterday he moved his finger
once

Stephen B. Wiley

Surc Signs

A hard-packed winter in Vermont
sharpens senses for signs of spring
not false signals from winter's tricks
but sure signs the herons will return

For the ear it's the fragile bells from the shore
as the melting shards of winter's iron coat
tinkle in chorus and fade away
driven against the shale by ripples returned

For the eye it's the storm of seedlings
from the cottonwood by the cabin
as they dance along the currents of the breeze

Stephen B. Wiley

PENULTIMATE

Nature paraphrases our scribbled texts
Our dime store joys and shrill suburban screams.
It bends trees and forks out lightning,
Buries Peruvian towns in mud,
Making mothers wail while no one listens;
Makes the earth gape wide to swallow a Ford.
We mutter meanwhile about our sad divorce,
And last year's suicides lie forgotten.

To our joys, a taste of simple honey,
Or the toaster free with our bank account,
Nature shouts ecstatic with the sunset,
Blue moon, or grand orgasmic rainbow.
Nature is the second-last yell of all,
Which our calamaties translate unto pygmy,
While we strut beneath the waving oaks,
Licking a purple lollipop.

Paul D. McGlynn

A Camel on the Highway

Near Al Dhirab,
southwest of Riyadh
we had a satellite site
for the TEP 6 phone project

Every morning,
leaving the crazy city
I passed the 'Riyadh River',
the overflow of the wastewater plant,
meandering 100 miles
into the desert,
disappearing.

Saudi Arabia,
we had two years time
to get used to
the muazzin's call,
the cruel beheadings,
the wonderful camels.

Near Al Dhirab,
one morning,
the traffic had to stop
because of a herd of camels,
passing the highway.

I watched the beautiful beasts,
following one of the ancient paths.
They walked their way
and at the end, a baby camel
following the herd.

For a short while
in the middle of the desert,
all rush, all madness, all busyness
came to a stand still.

Winfried Krepf

Dragonflies

casting their spawning rings on the water,
seldom see the fish they waken below.

The Pin

...so simple to discard, or bend,
turning up unexpectedly
shows forceful assertion for having been mislaid.

The Drip

Phantom reminder of a season wished bygone;
perching at nose tip—
returning as thoughts left unfinished.

Amuse a Muse

In mortal conflict,
the fitted form does contradict.

Craig M. Szwed

Plum Blossoms

Outside our door
Near the loading dock,
A pair of trees have filled with blossoms.

The scent fills you as you pass
Until you must for a moment
Be a blossom, be spring.

Mark Woodhouse

Snow

And the ground could be covered till March.
The river hasn't frozen yet this season
But now it will,
Now it will groan
And crack in the night
And the air itself will threaten
To turn steely solid,
An air in which even the light of the moon stops,
A white crescent the color of coconut
On the feathered stream.

Mark Woodhouse

Marrow

Nothing less than survival
A clean break
And the center sought with a hungry tongue.

Who has given
And who has taken
Can't be said.

Clear water runs over old, old stones
Taking a little with it
To the earth,
To the air,
To the sea.

Mark Woodhouse

A Band of Angels

Flying in
on final approach,
I could swear
I glimpsed a band of angels
floating on a wisp
of white mist, too ethereal to imagine
dressed in sun-stitched golden daylight
throwing up their hands
like harps,
despairing that in the roar
of jet engines,
their songs would never
get to be heard
by dispirited passengers,
about to land at Chicago's
hub of baggage handlers
beeping cabs
and the single and collective
souls' confusion

Arthur Gottlieb

DE FINITIONS

despair: de fifth tire.
décor: de apple's center.
depend: where de pool's bottom lies farthest down.
dependant: de ornament attached to de necklace.
descent: de smell.
debate: what de fish bite.
deliver: de meat you eat with onions.
denial: a river in Egypt.
depililatory: where you keep the asprin.
detail: what de dog wags.
deploy: de stratagem.
defer: de soft hair of a rich lady's coat.
devote: what gets us our Presidents.
despise: de CIA agents.
default: what, dear Brutus, lies not in our stars.
deduce: de lowest card in de deck.
deceit: a place to sit.
demote: de water-filled ditch around de castle.
defile: de dossier.
define: what de parking ticket makes you pay.
denote: de short letter.
detour: de guided way to see de place.
detritus: de dissertation.
depart: what de actor plays.
demure: de cat.
deride: what you buy de roller-coaster ticket for.
defeat: de raison d'etre for shoes.
defense: what keeps in de cows.
depose: de model's stance.
delight: an antonym for de heavy.
defame: what de publicity gets you.
despite: de grudge.
devoid: de emptiness.
debunk: where de cowboy slumbers.
detest: what I flunked yesterday.

William Woodruff

Beyond Ontology

What is it
that makes existence
what it is?

Everything
that doesn't make it
what it isn't.

William Woodruff

Tears

Each day that you had been gone
The tears in my ducts
Kept rising
Until they came crashing
Through
Pounding my tongue with salt.

Don A. Ryan

A Hole In The Air

We stand by
as the huge wrecking ball
slaps the face of a building
like an angry parent.

Window frames collapse
as if from fright
before the ball even makes contact.
Followed by the powdery surrender
of hundreds of bricks.

As we stare
mesmerized by such a display
of brute force.

A once proud building
falling to its knees
abjectly.
No one to speak up for it,
no time to say a prayer.

This building stood
on this spot
steadfast
reliable
through wind and storms.

Now there's a hole in the air,
not even a shadow to remind us.

Alan Harawitz

Fur And Feathers

I'm tying bass flies,
painting and coating them
with epoxy,
giving them a sheen like flesh.

Creatures of fur and feathers:
pride to make me burst
they look so real,
each one a small work of art.

Frog of closed-cell foam;
silver minnow tied with white marabou;
black smoky strips of rabbit fur
eager to shimmer their way
through blue water,
tempting and sensuous,
irresistible to both large and smallmouth bass.

It's all I can do to sit here
in the middle of winter
waiting for spring to bloom
like a flower.

Alan Harawitz

Reflecting on *Nature*

Emerson was
not a scientist,
he only understood
human machinery
(even then, the
inward funeral
was glorious).
His only sin
was being a writer
dissolved by the
oceans he found

in rain, by the pines
carried to his wake.
He chose the cross
in the middle,
identical with God,
sooner blind than lost

Scot Ehrhardt

From The Hospital Room

I'm falling asleep in this hospital room.
Here in this chair, receiving my weight
I sleep then contemplate.
Not now, in this room again,
as I close and open my eyes
till almost the end of the day.
But I stay. I stay in this chair.

Above the cross-beamed window
a large glass pane
offers a view outside.
A crane, a crisscross structure of steel
with a scissor-like bend midway
creates angles like those on a chalkboard.
Who directs, controls those gates?

The crane pokes unbidden, unable to fly.
Crooked into half its length,
balancing one-legged, in unbroken height.
What is it building, soundless to me
in this sealed room, awash in white?

Jodie S. Holmberg

Out on a High Note

By late afternoon tired.
Thoughts are fuzzy and
enervation sets in.

There is no treatment.
There is no cure.
One goes on living.

Enter into it.
Seek its depths.
Rise out of the cellar.

Loss is the feeling.
Faith is absent.
The soul is crushed.

Seclusion and time
are my friends, for now
Out on a high note.

Aaron W. Hillman

Middle Night Courage Needed

Know that there's only one low-watt
bulb crouching up inside my pullchain
lamp. How it strains to chew away some
smidgen of surrounding roomdark.
Listening close, you might hear its
valiantness-for-its-size penetrating
out into sections of the blackest
speckles swarming in to surround it.

Pressuring shadow morphs that do
seem snarly stubborn. Ever angrily
swirling back, determined to overwhelm
my little dim-glo bulb, break its
spirit.
And right from the veryinstant of
my switching it on, Bad-Old-Blackness
has flexed its long shadowed other self.
Seeming much more than just-somewhat
disturbed out there...

Jim DeWitt

Let Today Be The Time

I can carve with sunlight...
let me burn my thoughts into any wood
for as long as the clouds hold off.
Be the medium for
The Great Eye Of Day
to scorch black lines in tune with
my hand's command.
Creating scintillate detail in a face
or perform forth the power
of a unicorn's stance...
whatever it be, projecting the pulsed poetry
my soul has kept in store.
Depending only on whipping whims
yea moods of the "what"
whoever I've spoken to has said.
Seen simply thru those brain fumes
generated by a morning coffee's scent uprisen.
Oh sunlight so celestial
my right arm is your willing vehicle...
make me go on effervescing
forever for thee.

Jim DeWitt

Hindsight

I know a dog who goes through life
chasing his own hind end.
He always finds himself in circles,
and the object of his affection
is always just out of reach.
If he manages a nip,
he feels both pain and success
in bewilderment.
Blaming his object for his pain,
he chases faster and fiercer,
this time seeking revenge.

Always at opposite ends,
the dog and his object
constantly face each other,
though they seldom meet.
And his destiny is to seek till doomsday
something ridiculously more tangible
than dreams and rainbows.

Helen Shulman

Haiku

1

Lone yogi
sitting in the sand, without tide
there is no sailing

2

Snow falls
cold and silent. Everywhere
the beauty of crystals.

3

Saint and Satan
wrestling in the desert
two millenniums: everywhere dust!

4

Suns rise and set
and rains pass. My little boat
awaits its next journey

5

Thirty years
riding the evening train
And now your hair is white

Helen Shulman

The Soldier

Strike no bands,
fly no flags for me.
Forge my medals
into burnished troughs,
brimming with crème
for the starving swollen bellies.
I did no more than many —
except come home

John E. Hunt

Gifts

None have seen what I
have seen, flames in gold and silver
touched what I
have touched, the heat so close but
not burning me in that war.
No one has walked my mile,
travelers though there be.

I am more than the flow of family blood,
though it flows in rain and light;
more than the surroundings
that have gulped me up, somehow.

I can see what
you can not see, per chance,
the sacred is no mystery
to me either;
hear what you cannot hear, perhaps,
(there are bells in the tree tonight),
touch what you cannot touch,
the slain were there
no ornaments, you know.

Just one of the essential —
counted or not.

John E. Hunt

"He has the last word. He has the word"
–Atwood

Loss of Words

It seems as if he only
has words that can be heard.

Maybe it's me,
choosing to be quiet.
There is a power in silence
in the absence of sound.

No, even when I speak
he doesn't hear.

But he is not the only one.
In a group, in a crowd of them,
I become lost within icy tides
within swirls.

Where do all my words go?

They seem to drift and drown
into streams of melted snow.

Longing for the Sea

If I could see you once more,
I'd say all the the things
I always wanted to say...

once more turns into again
and again,
yet to never quite...

Like walking in deep water
or even just trying
to get to the ocean.

Jillian Foster Knight

Primitive Fires

When the world was still flat the horizon was
the matador's cape, evasive and mocking our
ignorance as we tested the waters of immortality
Excited by their songs we shouted at the birds
Sleeping with a splintered calm, the stars like
limbs outspread surrendered their dreams

Fire caused the uprising — our first rebellion
The scent of smoke making our hearts beat faster
So we gathered wood to give the breath of fire
a roaring voice, to scare away our demons
From our warm caves we outlasted the Ice Age

We picked berries — that sweetness staining the
wicked lust of our throat
Today, we are that truth — the fruit born from the
roots of flowers that we tasted so long ago —

Asleep by the fireplace, the machine of night spins
like a giant flywheel   In the mills' molten steel
slashes like glowing sabers into the huge eye of night
In our dreams we worship the magic of fire as it burns
the pages of tomorrow
Unaware that our children are dancing in its flames

Vladimir Swirynsky

Exact Moments of Time

Falling rain breaks the stillness
Of the countryside, strangely beneath an electric sky.
Morning is cold.

All new things begin exact moments of time.
And I am thinking of a day or any other day
Over the years
Where two people lived, as if in a magic moment
Smiling, laughing, even shouting...

And afterwards that mild falling under the air's motion
Quietly breathing a day of spring.

Then, there is past —
That whirling emotion caught in my throat —
That foundation from which I operate in the present

Hearing the rain falling, thinking of a day
Where rain stippled our pond.

Here you lived — lived both of us splashing one moment to the next
Like two goldfish in a crystal vase...or because

There was no vase to save us
Two slippery fishes in a poem of memory and loss.

In the distance a dog barks.

And I am missing the sound of your breath.

Betty Ann Whitney

Deeper Than an Eye Can Know

How easy it is for me
to want to comfort you
on days drifting dark circles, like smoke
on your skin — deeper than an eye can know.

No one should have to focus on so much negation.

We are connected through eyes that see
rather than merely sense another.
From image to thought, the sparkle of life
returns life to us, again and again

and again...

as if from a spell of blindness.

Betty Ann Whitney

Ballet of Shadows

It is difficult to sleep at night. They're here with me,
always in the dark. Numbers change in funeralistic time...
on and on and on and on ... water torture would be
paradise. Images materialize in the sheet rock of my walls.
My ghostly companions rip at the frayed seams
of my sanity. Sun rise, tender sun rise, rejuvenate me anew
for another day.

Vincenzo J. Macrino

Portrait of the Mother

Out of the dark canvas of her smile
flows fisherman's lace,
a hairnet for a weary lady
draped
in gracious folds about her stateliness.
Her chain sits near windows
without glass, her face bejewelled
by saffron
segments of the sun.
Walls, their broken parts are speechless;
she is webbed within a solitary
gaze,
given to the catatonic ease of the
painter's stain.
She says everything through the dark moments
of her eyes;
her smile covers us in veins woven
to gather fish
from souls that oceans made to adore her.

Mary Rudbeck Stanko

A Poem in the Making

I looked for you under a rock
in the flower-filled garden
behind the house. When you
weren't there, I went to the park
and looked for you some more.
I looked in the short green grass
and the tall woody grass. I looked
in the shallow waters of the pond
where mallard ducks
peacefully swam. I stopped
at the gazebo and looked across the bay.
I walked over to the mighty oaks
and the royal palms hoping
to find you there. Then I heard the birds
and stopped to see if their coos
and tweets would bring me closer
to you. I looked and looked and searched
all day. When I could search no longer,
I finally stopped. Exhausted
I went home and fell asleep. It was then
that you finally found me.

Benita Glickman

Fishing for the Past
(for Barry)

Casting his line
The man stands
On the edge
Of a lake so tainted
Only the desperate
Would eat the fish
Bellies bloated
Riddled with pesticides

The sun spots glisten
On water deceptively blue
And the sky is pink with morning
The man lives
In a world of memories
And he remembers the glacial taste
When he drank from a running stream

Casting his line
He ignores the honking cars
Joggers sweating on the road
And the occasional walker
Who wonders why
He fishes in polluted water

Casting his line
He questions whether
The catching of fish or
The stillness of time
Snares his desire
To escape into the past
And he never gazes
At his watch until
He puts the bait back in the box
And walks towards the 21st century

Phyliss L. Geller

Cross Ventilation

On those hot summer nights
when her breath could not escape
and money was only exchanged
in a game of monopoly;
she would lie in her bed sweating,
beads dripping down her face
not yet lined by years...
still the secrets existed.

Her father would say
"open the shades,
there is cross ventilation"
By morning
the breeze would flap clothing
hung on a line
strung from kitchen to bedroom windows,
still she could barely breathe.

During the summer
there was always the cold, clear water
of Long Island Sound
to escape the heat of August.
She would hitchhike to the beach
swim for miles in saline green,
pretending her feet could grow fins
that she could remain submerged
coming up for air only to lure
a sailor from a ship.

On weekdays,
She would watch her mother
scrub clothing on an old washboard;
the smell of soap filling the room.
Then everything was hung on the line
to dry in the warmth of the sun.

At times, she would pray
her soul could be washed too,
hung on the clothes line
next to the white cotton shirt;
its secrets bleached by the sun and
evanesced into its light.
Then she would lie in her bed...breathe;
welcome a kaleidoscope of dreams,
the open shades giving
the cross ventilation permission;
no longer dreading the summer nights.

Phyliss L. Geller

The Poets

Craig Arnel is from Long Island, New York. He pursued his dreams of having an independent music career playing solo guitar and writing lyrics. His poems have appeared in various anthologies and literary journals. He is a member of Poets of the Palm Beaches.

Barry Ballard is the recipient of the *Explorations Award for Literature* from the University of Alaska and the *Boswell Poetry Prize*. He has also published four award winning chapbook collections.

Jackie Bartley's poems have appeared in a number of Journals including *Iron Horse Literary Review*, *Phoebe*, and *The Spoon River Review*. Her first full length collection, *Bloodroot*, was recently published.

Therese Bearse has had work in many journals among which are *The Kaleidoscope Review*, *The Blind Mans Review Anthology* and others. Her work will be coming up in *The Mid America Poetry Review*, *Elements Magazine*, *The Rockford Review* and other publications.

Louis E. Bourgeois received a B.A. in English from the *Louisiana State University*. This year he was the first graduate of the University of Mississippi's new MFA Program in Creative Writing. He is an instructor of English at the University of Mississippi in Oxford. His poems have appeared in America and Europe in such journals as *Poetic Hours*, *Parnassus*, *The Oxford American* and *Tundra*. He has a chap book coming out this spring entitled *Through the Cemetary Gates*.

Anselm Brocki has written over 2,200 poems and has had over 915 poems accepted by over 540 publications, among them: *The Amherst Review*, *Maryland Poetry Review*, *Piedmont Literary Review* and *Walts Corner*. He has also had a paperback of 100 poems entitled *Mornings at the All-Nite*. He was a senior editor for *Houghton Mifflin* and currently runs his own editing business.

John Michael Buscemi was born in Saddle River, N.J. He graduated Ramapo High School in June 2000. He enlisted in the U. S. Army in August 2000. He was injured in April 2000 in Airborne School and was medically discharged from the Army in November 2002 and currently lives in Florida.

Jamie Cavanagh has had work in *Edgz*, *Axe Factory* and *Struggle*.

Kent Clair Chamberlain was born in Dickonson County Seat of Abelene, Kansas. He attended *Southern Oregon College*. He has been writing poetry since 1961.

Lee Chanin works in financial services. She is blessed with two great children who are devoted to her and enjoys a healthy and happy life. Lee writes short stories as well.

Robert Cooperman has had his latest collection *The Widow's Burden* as a finalist for *Foreward Magazines Book of the Year*. His *In the Colorado Gold Fever Mountains* won the Colorado Book Award for Poetry in 2000. His work has appeared in *Mississippi Review*, *The American Poetry Review* and *Slant*.

James DeWitt is the editor of *Eschew Obfuscation Review*. He is the author of 34 published books. His work has appeared in 1902 literary reviews.

Richard Dinges Jr. has a M.A. in Literary Studies from the University of Iowa. His poems have appeared or will appear in *Connecticut River Review*, *Iconoclast*, *Pegasus* and *Seattle Review*.

Riva Dunaief has been writing poetry always. She is a member of the Poets of the Palm Beaches.

Scot Ehrhardt studies Teacher Education at the University of Dayton (Ohio) where he is the Assistant Editor for *Orpheus*, their literary and visual arts magazine. His work has appeared in *Nexus*, *Artspike* and *The Black Perspective* and will be in *Our Time is Now*, a publication of Dayton Public Schools.

Brian C. Felder most recently published in *Miller's Pond* and *The Unknown Writer*, is an established poet with nationwide credits.

Elizabeth G. Fleischman is the recipient of the George Jones Creative Writing Award, and a semi-finalist in the National Novel- in-Progress Competition. Two poems, now songs, are registered BMI.

Zan Gay is a reference librarian who advocates for young adults with mental retardation. Her work has appeared in various literary journals. Her short story placed first in the *2002 South Writers Network Contest* and her poetry shared First Prize in *The Adams Rib Project 2002*, read at the *Harriet Himmel Gilman Theatre* in West Palm Beach, FL.

Phyliss Geller is the publisher and editor of the Meridian Anthology, and a member of The Poets of the Palm Beaches. She has been writing poetry since 1974, and her work has appeared in Poetry Journals. Her most recent credit is Pegasus. Ms. Geller is a member of the Poets of the Palm Beaches, and the Florida State Poets Association/The National Federation of the State Poetry Societies. She is also a practicing Psychotherapist.

Benita Glickman is a recipient of *The Alice Minnie Hertz Heniger Award for Children's Literature* from Lehman College. She has won poetry contests through *The Riverdale Press* and *ValueVision*. Her poems have been published in many journals and her short story, *A Childhood Memory*, appeared in *Chicken Soup for the Sister's Soul.*

Arthur Gottlieb is a poet from Oregon whose work has appeared in *The Ledge*, *Chiron Review*, *The Alembic* and others.

John Grey has appeared in *South Carolina Review*, *Peregrine*, *Bellevue Literary Review* and is upcoming in *Pennsylvania English* and *New Laurel Review*.

Alan Harawitz is a retired New York City middle school teacher. He lives nine months of the year in Brooklyn, N.Y. and the remainder in Central Maine, where he enjoys fishing. His poems have appeared in *Rattle Pivot*, *Red Wheelbarrow* and other journals.

Pier Hart is a native Oregonian, now living in Pennsylvania. Ms. Hart intends to go into a career in medicine.

Aaron W. Hillman is the author of the book *I Was Born, See...* his work has appeared in *Palo Alto Review*, *The University of Houston Forum*, *The Hartford Courant*, *The Santa Barbara Book Review*, among others.

Glenna Holloway has had work appear in the *Pushcart Price 2001*, *Western Humanities Review*, *The Georgia Review*, *Michigan Quarterly Review*, *Notre Dame Review*, *The Formalist*, *The Southern Poetry Review* and many others.

Jodie S. Holmberg holds an M.F.A. in writing from Vermont College. She's been published in two anthologies and wrote the liner notes for the CD, *Songs We Sang*.

John E. Hunt has had his work appear in *Reflections*. He has a B. S. Degree in Psychology and has worked mostly in the human service field.

Stacie M. Kiner was the recipient of the Hannah Kahn Memorial Award for 1999. Her work has appeared in many publications including *The Southeast Review*, *The Comstock Review*, *Sun Dog*, *The Charlotte Poetry Review*, *The Madison Review*, and *The Apalachee Quarterly*. Ms. Kiner is the co-founder of the *Beach Road Poetry Workshop.*

Jillian Foster Knight When not writing, Ms. Knight is a sutler at Scottish Festivals, Rendezvous and other Living History events across the country. Her work has appeared in various literary journals.

Stephen Kopel is a teacher, cyclist, dancer and art collector. he has published in *Skylark*, *Haight Ashbury Journal* and *Comstock.* His book *Crux* was published in 2001. He was a nominee for San Francisco Poet Laureate 2002/2003.

Marylin Krepf is the Literary Editor of the *Meridian Anthology*. She is the author of *Half Past Sunset*, a collection of poems, which was favorably reviewed by both *Publisher's Weekly* and *Library Journal*. Her work has appeared in many journals and she is the recipient of several awards. She is a member of the Florida State Poets Association/National Federation of the State Poetry Societies. Ms. Krepf teaches poetry at the prestigious Royal Palm Academy in Naples, Florida, and is an editor.

Winfried Krepf is a German engineer living in Naples, FL. He was the editor of two newspapers. He lived in several countries, among them Saudi Arabia, which was the inspiration for his poem.

Gilda Kreuter has published four books of poetry. Her poems have appeared in many anthologies and journals. She was the winner of the 2000 and 2001 *Chapbook Contest* sponsored by the *Poets of the Palm Beaches*. Her books were chosen to be presented at the Author's Showcase at the *Delray Beach Public Library*.

Pete Lee has had poetry published in *Creosote*, *Other Voices*, *Verandah* and elsewhere. He has worked as a newspaper reporter, private investigator, federal intelligence operations specialist, and U.S. Army Sergeant/Counterintelligence Agent.

Kathy Macdonald writes young adult and adult fiction. She is a member of the invitation-only writing group mentored by the award winning Joyce Sweeney.

Vincenzo J. Macrino is a police officer with many publishing credits, among which are *Maelstrom*, *Poetic Voices Magazine*, *Apropos* and others.

Barney F. McClelland has published numerous short stories, articles and poems on both sides of the Atlantic. These publications include *Acorn* (Dublin Writers Group), *Oxford Magazines* and others. He has two chapbooks: *In the Field of my Heart* and *Casual Cruelties*.

Paul D. McGlynn taught creative writing at Eastern Michiga University. His chapbook *Magical Regression* was published ... 1993. He has two poems nominated for the *Pushcart Prize* and his work has appeared in over 170 journals in the U.S., Canada, Australia and Great Britain.

Rochelle Hope Mehr has appeared in two anthologies, *The World Healing Book* and *The Book of Hope*, as well as numerous other journals and publications.

Vladimir Orlov lives in Volgograd, Russia. Since 1992 his work has appeared in more than fifty Literary Journals, in the U.S., U.K., and Australia.

June Owens has published many poems and won many prizes. She is the author of *Tree Line* and the winner of the *Sparrowgrass Poet of the Year Award.* Her book is available by writing to J. Owens, 5545 Meadowbrook Ave., Zephyrhills, FL 33541.

Don A. Ryan is a High School teacher in Chicago. He is a member of the *Academy of American Poets*, and the author of a chapbook entitled *The Final Moments*. His poetry has appeared in *Mid America Poetry Review*, *Maelstrom* and other literary journals.

Helen Schulman was born in New York City. She received a B.A. in English from City College of New York and holds a Masters Degree in Social Work from New York University. She has edited textbooks and Ph.D. dissertations at Western Reserve University in Cleveland, OH.

Brenda Serotte teaches Writing and Literature at *Nova Southeastern University* in Ft. Lauderdale, FL. Her work has appeared in *The Atlanta Review*, the anthology *Literature: An Introduction to Reading and Writing* and various other literary journals.

Lucille Gang Shulklapper is a workshop leader for the Council of Florida Libraries. Her fiction and poetry has appeared in *Slant*, *Switched-on* and *Into the Teeth of the Wind*. Her first chapbook of poems *What You Cannot Have* has recently been published.

Virginia Artrip Snyder is an award winning reporter. She was a private investigator for 22 years. She is a member of the National league of American Pen Women.

Mary Rudbeck Stanko is the author of *Eavesdropping*. She is now living in Canada.

Richard St. John has had his work appear in *Carolina Quarterly*, *Great Lakes Review*, *Sewanee Review* and other publications. He studied English at Princeton University (B.A.) and the University of Virginia (M.A.). He is initiating a project called 'Conversations for Common Wealth'.

Edward Michael O'Durr-Supranowicz has had poems in *Rattle*, *Black Mountain Review* (Northern Ireland) and other journals.

Vladimir Swirynsky was nominated for the 2002 Pushcart Prize. He has published eight books in a span of seven years. His book *This Tear in My Poem* has just been published. His work has appeared in many journals.

Craig M. Szwed has been published in *Once Upon a World* and in two anthologies compiled by *The International Library – Library of Poetry*. He has published *American Haiku* on compact disc.

Colleen Ann Traphagen has been published in *The Story Teller*, *Footprints*, *Offerings*, as well as many others. One of her stories was published in the best selling book *Small Miracles for Women*.

Betty Ann Whitney is a poet, fiction writer, and artist, and has been writing over the last decade. Ms. Whitney's recent work has appeared in numerous literary magazines and collections of poetry, including a short story in *Galaxy Literary Journal*.

Stephen B. Wiley, after 50 years of practicing law, was drawn to poetry. He has been published in various journals.

Mark Woodhouse has had his work in a number of publications including *The Gettysberg Review*, *The Maryland Poetry Review*, *Lucid Moon* and *The American Poetry Monthly*. He is a librarian at Elmira College and a sometimes drummer.

William Woodruff has had poems in various literary publications including *Chaminade Literary Review*, *Aura Literary Arts Review*, *Chase Park*, *Fox Cry*, and *The Haiku Quarterly*.

Cherise Wyneken has appeared in a variety of journals, periodicals and anthologies. She is the author of *Seeded Puffs*, a collection of poems.

Gerald Zipper is the author of *Wounded Hopes*, a collection of poetry. He was named one of New Jersey's top 50 poets for 2002. He was appointed 'Consultant on the Arts' to the New York State Senate. His poetry has appeared in over 200 poetry, literary and University publications throughout the U. S. and Canada.